Pier Paol

The Cello and its history

New English edition 27 Feb 2020

Pier Paolo Maccarrone

The Cello and its history

New English edition 27 Feb 2020

PREMISE

The cello is an instrument that has always fascinated the listener and the student for his sound. In fact it is often preferred over other musical instruments. The purpose of this book is to provide information on the history and repertoire dedicated to this instrument. For the cello they wrote all the greatest composers from J. S. Bach to L. Berio. I know that to treat such a vast subject would require hundreds of pages so the reader will excuse me right now if he will find the present volume not entirely exhaustive. In the bibliography I have reported the books that I recommend to read to those who want to know more about this magical instrument. Enjoy the reading.

Pier Paolo Maccarron

e

THE CELLO

THE CLASSIFICATION

The cello is a musical instrument from the group of string chordophones, it has four strings, tuned at the right fifth intervals. It is part of the subfamily of the "violins", which includes those instruments with four strings, tuned at fifth intervals, which have "effe" cuts on the soundboard (or harmonic plane). The subfamily of the "violins" thus differs from the subfamily of the "violas" which instead includes antique instruments with "C" cuts, tuned for fourths and thirds, with strings in a variable number from three, to seven or more and equipped on the keyboard of frets.

The tuning of the four strings corresponds to that of the viola do-sol-re-la but a lower octave. Cello writing given the its remarkable extension (6 octaves) is carried out with the help of three keys: of bass for the low register, of tenor for the middle register, of violin for the high register. Rarely, in some manuscripts of music from the Baroque period, some composers such as J. S. Bach use the contralto key (manuscript of the prelude to the VI suite for cello solo).

History

While the violin, complete in all its essential aspects, appeared for the first time in representation between the end of the twelfth and the beginning of the thirteenth century, the "bass violin", what today we would call the cello, only appeared in the fifteenth century. Its rather late appearance is due to the Western sound ideal of the Middle Ages, which remains until the fifteenth century, and prefers a kind of high-pitched, nasal sound. The singers used the voice so that today we would say oriental, and the instruments that accompanied the singing (because this was their main function) had to produce a similar sound. At that time the low voice was not part of our musical conception.

From the middle of the fifteenth century, some composers of the Flemish school began to widen the vocal range downwards until they reached Do grave, where it remained for practical reasons until today.

The cello was born in Italy in the second half of the XVI century. The cello structurally does not differ from the violin if we exclude the tip of wood, metal or carbon fiber, called tip, of variable length, which applied to the lower band of the cello constitutes its point of support, keeping it raised from the ground. The ferrule was applied to the instrument only in the sec. XIX from the famous Belgian cellist François Servais **1.**

The cello is played while sitting holding the instrument between the legs, resting on the tip. The performer moves the bow crosswise on the strings. The bow is made to slide on the strings, the fingers of the left hand can act on the keyboard by pressing on the strings to decrease the length, thus modifying the frequency of the sound obtained. Like the other string instruments, the cello can also be pinched both with the right hand and the left hand.

The cello produces a very rich sound in harmonics, with a dark and deep timbre. It has the most serious sound among the instruments of the string quartet and produces a sound very close to the human voice.

The cellos made in the Baroque period were larger than the current ones. The luthiers began producing smaller ones around 1690, but were not accepted until the middle of the following century. Smaller tools were useful for reducing the tension of the left hand.

Cello and violin making

Great luthiers such as A. Amati, Maggini and Gaspare da Salò from 1550 to 1600 created magnificent examples of cellos. Even the great Stradivari devised some in which the sound box measured 79 cm in length; subsequently it reduced it to 75 cm, universally accepted dimension, and diapason related to the length with a cello-diapason ratio of about 54/100.

Some measurements of the Stradivarius cellos are:

* Medicean 79.7 cm diap. 43.2 year of construction 1690

* Servais 79.2 cm diap. 42.8 year of construction 1701

* Bläss 75.9 cm diap. 40.6 year of construction 1698

* Duport 75 cm diap. 40 year of construction 1711

Towards the end of his production, Stradivarius fixed the modern measurements, that is, the length 75, tuning fork 40 / 40.5, handle 28 from the nut to the band, with an excavation of 25 cm from the curve of the 1/2 position to the curve of the fourth position.

The cello by A. Stradivari are authentic masterpieces, even more rare than the violins of the same master. The number of Stradivari's "celli" of established attribution does not exceed thirty in the whole world. Among these, the former Baron Rothschild of Rocco Filippini, the former Davidoff of Yo-Yo Ma and belonging years ago to Jacheline Duprè, the Duport by Mstislav Rostropovich, the Servais of Anner Bylsma, are undoubtedly the best known to the general public.

To loosen the tension of the strings on the soundboard and allow the jumper to have a looser vibration, today the nose of the handle is built higher, bringing the attachment to the upper plinth, including the 30-34 mm keyboard, which is equivalent to thickness of the thumb of the hand that must pass freely under the keyboard. This serves to reduce the angle that the strings form on the bridge and therefore the decrease in pressure on the soundboard to the advantage of sound. The raising of the nut above by a few millimeters also serves the aforementioned purpose.

The measures of the modern cello are:

• length of the handle from the nut to the edge

of the soundboard: 28 cm

• keyboard length: 58.5 cm

• height of the keyboard to the soundboard

    of the upper block: 2.5 / 2.7 cm

• height between the inside edge of the keyboard and the

 soundboard: 5 / 6.5 cm

• tuning fork: 40-40.5 cm

• thickness of the handle from the nut: 2.7 cm

• body length from edge to edge: 75 cm

• thickness of the handle at the fourth position: 3.1 cm

• height of the band: 12 cm

Other memorable and illustrious luthiers who built and built cellos for over 400 years, especially in Italy, were: N. and G. Amati, J. Stainer, C. Bergonzi, G.P. and P. Maggini, G. Guarneri del Gesù, G. B Guadagnini, A. and N. Gagliano, A and G. Grancino, D. Montagnana, C. Oddone, GB Rogeri, G. and F. Tononi, R and G. Antoniazzi, M. Goffriller, A. Pollastri, C. Testore, GB Vuillame, L. Bisiach, D. Tecchler, B. Carlson, G. Dindo etc.

The etymology

The name is of Italian origin and could indicate "small violone **2.**[1]" but the etymology is much debated. Initially used as a substitute for the viola da gamba, the instrument was officially mentioned with the term violoncino **3.** in 1641, in a collection of sonatas G. B. Fontana **4.**

The violoncini, unfortunately, being exchanged in the following centuries for Celli 3/4 studio, were enlarged, modified and therefore lost.

The measures of the violone were the following:

* length from edge to edge: 69 cm

* upper width: 33.5 cm

* lower width: 42 cm

* tuning fork: 38.5 cm

* height of the bands: 11.5 cm

* length of the handle: 28.5 cm

* height of the curl   20.5 cm

As you can see, these are the measures of a modern 3/4 cello. The violone fell into disuse in the 1700s and then, other confusions were generated, because many scholars confused it with the small cello built by Bach for his cantatas and for the VI Suite in re magg BWV 1012 for solo cello **5.**

This small cello could be mounted on four or five strings. In fact Bach, with the great precision used in composing his works, specifies the four-string cello tuning in the fifth suite in Do-Sol-Re-Sol, then for small five-stringed cello in the sixth suite in Do-Sol- La-Re-Mi.

Moreover, even today, the indication concerning the orchestration of some works of the XVI century is debated. In 1607 C. Monteverdi, in his work Orpheus, orchestrates the instrumental part for ten "violas da braccio" with five voices from the bass to the soprano, so that we can hypothesize from then on the presence in the violas from arm to bass of cello-like ancestors from we known. Marin Mersenne **6.** in 1636 states that the famous 24 violins of the King consisted of six sopranos, six basses, four highs, four tenors, and four "quinton".

Is Quinton an uncertain term, perhaps an ancestor of the current cello? The name may refer to the five-string bass violin tuned like the cello, with an extra string intoned a fifth below the lower string. M. Praetorius, in 1619, seems to confirm the existence of such an instrument, counting it among the violets from the arm with fa-do-sol-re-la tuning which he called "Gross Quint-Bass".

Since the tuning of the "Gross Quint-Bass" is the same as that of the modern cello, except for the fifth string, it is clear that Praetorius in his Syntagma Musicum (1619) did not foresee the existence of a double-bass instrument. Furthermore, the tuning by fifth also excludes the possibility that an instrument thus made could play an octave below.

From some sources it is possible to see the existence of instruments that were played like the modern cello but tied around the chest. This is due to the concept of an "arm" instrument.

So we can say that the bass violin was a "viola da braccio", and therefore had to rest on the arm, or at least be played in a position similar to this one, given the size of the instrument. In fact the small bass with smaller dimensions of the modern cello is plausible to have been played in that position, while the larger instrument was held vertically. Not infrequently in some representations even the latter are held horizontally so as to feed almost a sort of myth on the primordial position of the first cellos.

The element that generates further confusion is the finding of depictions of the medium bass violin, the nearest instrument in size to the modern cello, held in an oblique position.

An image depicting this position is visible in a fresco in the loggia of the chapel of Roccapietra near Varallo (Vercelli). On two opposite walls, two low violins are depicted, of which the largest is held in a vertical position, the smallest on the chest. Other paintings of the XVI century show that there was also another position, the oblique one. The instruments were suspended obliquely on the chest by means of a strap or ribbon. The instrument was called "viola da gamba", a further term that generated confusion in scholars. Probably with this expression he wanted to indicate: "a big stringed instrument held on the chest and suspended by means of a belt".

Antonio Stradivari
'De Munck' cello 1730

Differences between viola and cello

To explain the differences between the violins and the violas, I report some steps taken from the book Il Cello written by William Pleeth **7.**, which was illuminating for my training as a cellist. This valuable book contains the considerations provided by the great teacher W. Pleeth centered on the position, technique and interpretation of the cello, while Nona Pyron **8.** has edited a section devoted entirely to the history of the instrument, exploring in particular the oldest repertoire.

Mersenne **9.** is very precise when he describes the violins in his Harmonie Universelle (1636):

"The violin is one of the simplest instruments, in the sense that it has only four strings and has no frette on the handle. For this reason all the perfect consonances can be played on it, as with the voice, because the fingers can press the string in the desired point. This makes it more complete than the instruments with the hurries, where one is forced to use a temperament and to lower and grow most of the consonances, and alter all the intervals, as I will show later ... It should be noted that the violin is suitable for all genres of music, and that the enharmonic can be played on it, and all the species of the diatonic and chromatic (genre), because it has no hurries, and contains all imaginable intervals , which are potentially on the keyboard, and it is comparable to the primitive material capable of aggregating itself in every form, since there is no hurry on the violin that produce a particular sound. Thus it must be concluded that it contains an infinity of different tones, and that the rope like the straight line contains

an infinity of points ... "Continuing in his treatise to give a description of the viola he says **10.**:

> "*The parts of the viola are similar to those of the violin ... it differs ... only in the frette that limit its possibilities and, instead of the infinity that it could have, they establish seven or eight equal semitones marked on the handle from eight frette ...*

In addition, John Gunn, a century and a half later, publishes The Practice of Fingering the Violoncello and explains the reasons why the cello produces a more precise intonation than the violas and therefore is a more versatile instrument. In fact, he writes:

"(...) *The violin was much better suited to produce the right effect everywhere, due to the greater strength and brilliance of the sound; but it was found that, if placed in the hands of skilled artists, it could produce a more perfect harmony than was possible with violets. This stemmed from a cause, which was probably not previously suspected, that is, that the fingers, for study, and the guidance of a good ear, obtained a more accurate intonation than was ever possible from the indication of the hurries , fixed on the keyboard with the utmost mathematical precision. These can be placed so that the intervals are perfectly intoned, but only in one tone; in the others the intervals are very false; and if the difference were subdivided and masked by what we call temperament, the variation from the exact intonation would be easily distinguishable and offensive to a fine ear* ".

The actual cello was born at the moment when it ceased to be only the shoulder to the foot violone (now double bass).

Several scholars have shown that precisely in Bologna, around the chapel of San Petronio and at the Philharmonic Academy, the "Shoulder Cello to the modern" began its solo adventure. It is no coincidence that the first cello theorist is an Emilian virtuoso, the cornetist Father Bartolomeo Bismantova, a servant of Reggio Emilia but active in Ferrara, who in his Compendio Musicale, a manuscript dated 1667, dedicates a small chapter to the cello with the tuning for fifths except for the most serious note which, for executive convenience, recommends tuning in kings instead of do. In this period also the way of "arcing" will have evolved into that typical of the violin, in fact not infrequently in this period of transition many cellists will use the grip of the bow from viola da gamba, with the palm of the hand facing the high.

The cello in the society of the seventeenth century

The cello in the seventeenth century began to spread among the people of all walks of life who made music for their own pleasure. In the paintings we often see people from all social classes playing the cello, which highlights both the "amateurish" aspect and the pleasant situation recreated by chamber music. So the cellists get together to play in small groups with one or more violins or wind instruments. They also played alone, and even singing along with the instrument. Roger North, in his Memoirs of Music (1770 ca.), provides the following description of the cello:

> "*There was a society of gentlmen of good esteem ... that used to meet often for consort after Baptist's manner and exceedingly well with bass violin, their friends and acquaintances were admitted, and, by degrees, as the hunger of the meeting spreads, so many auditors came that their room, they took room in Fleet Street, and the* Taverner pretended to make formal seats, and to take money, and then the society disbanded. *".

> "*There was a company of esteemed gentlemen ... who used to meet for (playing) in consorts* **11.** *and because they played very well the bass violins (which was then a court instrument, and which they used to borrow), the their friends and acquaintances were admitted, and gradually, as the fame of these meetings spread, so many listeners flowed that the room*

*was packed, and to avoid this inconvenience they moved to
Fleet Street, and the owner wanted to put places for payment,
and so the company broke up. "*

The cello thus became an indispensable component in church and halls not only for groups of violins, but also for mixed groups of wind and string instruments. Many cellists, such as G. B. Vitali (died 1692), were highly esteemed as cellists also as composers. In fact almost all the performers of the seventeenth and eighteenth centuries they are both composers and performers.

History of the repertoire

To be honest, in dealing with the cello repertoire I have to face a thorny issue, that of the scarcity of music in the cellular repertoire of the seventeenth century when compared to the large quantity for violin. Two reasons can explain this difference. The first concerns the idiomatic writing for an instrument, the cello, which took its first steps; the second reason it concerns the consideration that the cellists, considering themselves "bass violin players" naturally adopted the violin repertoire (transported an octave below), without worrying about the difference in voice of the instruments, as singers often do with the solo repertoire. It also explains why the cello solos were written in violin key until the 19th century (see sonatas and quartets by Boccherini, Haydn, Beethoven, Mozart, etc.).

The cello knows its first period of luster and affirmation as a solo instrument in Italy, around 1650 thanks to Giovanni Battista Vitali, Violone player, with the Matches on different Sonatas. In Emilia with the Sinfonie a 2 by G. Bononcini **12.**, the Ricercari (1689-91) by D. Gabrielli **13.**, the sonatas and the chamber concerts by G. M. Jacchini **14.**, the Chamber Entertainment by A. M. Ariosti **15.** .

The technical resources of the instrument were further refined during the sec. XVIII through the sonatas of B. Marcello, E. F. Dall'Abaco, A. Vivaldi, L. Leo, G. Tartini, by G. Platti.

From the early years of the eighteenth century the music for cello increased dramatically; Sonatas, Concerts and other compositions spread rapidly and this led to the full emancipation of the cello from the violin.

Other composers who have written for cello are J. Barriere, whose Sonata in D major is known. (1733); S. Paxton of which the Sonata in re magg op. 1 n. 6 (ca 1760); G. B. Cervetto of which we know the Six Sonatas for cello and B. C. or Trii for three cellos or for two violins and bass; G. Valentini for the Sonata op. 8 n. 1 in major (1714); R. Lindley for the Three Duets for Two Cellos.

But the composer who certainly gave the greatest contribution to the solo cello repertoire is undoubtedly L. Boccherini. His sonatas for cello and B. C. op. 7, his concerts for cello and orchestra of which I want to mention a few such as: G 479, WV 480, G 481; duets for two cellos, string quartets, guitar quintets and symphonies represent masterpieces of rare beauty in which the cello expresses the vertexes of virtuosity and bel canto.

In the neoclassical period it was used, among others, by Franz Joseph Haydn and Ludwig van Beethoven. Haydn composed two wonderful concertos for cello and orchestra one in do magg. and the other in re major Hob. VIIb, n. 1 and 2. Beethoven who dedicated five sonatas for cello and piano to the cello from 1796 to 1815: op. 5 n. 1 in fa magg. and op. 5 n. 2 in sol min., Op. 69 in the major, op. 102 n. 1 in do magg. and op. 102 n. 2

in re magg .. Also Beethoven has composed three series of variations for cello and piano:

12 Variations on a theme from Handel's "Judas Maccabée" oratory; 7 variations on the theme "Bei Männern, welche Liebe fühlen" and 12 variations on the theme "Ein Mädchen oder Weibchen" from the "Magic Flute" by W. A. Mozart. Finally, beyond the string quartets from the six of the op. 18 until the last op. 131 and the eight Trios for violin, cello and piano of which we remember the op. 97 n. 1 "The spectra" and the op. 97 "The Archduke" in which the cello plays an important role is to remember the Triple Concerto for violin, cello, piano and orchestra op. 56 in do major. W. A. Mozart did not assign specific compositions to the cello, but to the violin, viola and cello for fun and to the string quartets dedicated to the Prussian king, called for this reason Prussian, the cello plays a solo instrument role. From the romanticism to the present day we must mention Robert Schumann, Franz Schubert, Felix Mendelssohn-Bartholdy, Frédéric Chopin, Johannes Brahms, Edward Elgar Edward Grieg, Max Bruch, Gabriel Fauré, Camille Saint-Saëns, Claude Debussy, Zoltán Kodály, Benjamin Britten, Pëtr Il'ič Čajkovskij, George Enescu, Antonín Dvořák, Ernest Bloch, Dmitry Dmitrievich Shostakovich, Frederich Delius, Paul Hindemith, Richard Strauss, Sergei Rachmaninov, Sergei Prokofiev, Francis Poulenc, Arthur Honneger, Bertold Hummel, Charles Villiers Stanford, Kurt Weill, Samuel Barber, John Ireland, Dmitri Kabalevsky,

Alfred Schnittke, Sofia Gubaidulina, Max Reger, Lowell Liebermann, H. Villa Lobos, Joaquin Rodrigo, Iannis Xenakis, Astor Piazzolla, Luigi Dallapiccola, Luciano Berio, etc.

R. Schumann composed the Fünf Stüke in Volkston op. 102 for cello and piano; the Adagio and Allegro in the B flat magg. Op. 70 for cello and piano (orig. For horn and piano); and the famous Concerto for cello and orchestra in the min.

F. Schubert has composed a musical moment op. 94 n. 3 for cello and piano; a Sonata for cello and piano "Arpeggione" in the min D. 821 for cello and piano which is recognized as one of the masterpieces of the chamber repertoire. Also F. Mendelssohn-Bartholdy has composed two sonatas for cello and piano op. 45 in si bem. Maj. and op. 58 in major; the Variations Concertanti for cello and piano op. 17 and the Lied ohne worte op. 109. F. Chopin has dedicated a splendid sonata for cello and piano op. 65 in sol min and it is significant that it is the only sonata for duo of his chamber music production. J. Brahms has given us two beautiful Sonatas for cello and piano op. 36 and op. 64. E. Elgar wrote the Adagio for cello (viola) and piano "Sospiri" op. 70, the Concerto for cello and orchestra in mi mi. op. 85. Eduard Grieg has composed a Sonata for cello and piano op. 36 in A minor. G. Faurè has composed two sonatas for cello and piano op. 109 in re min. and op. 117 in sol min. M. Bruch composed Kol Nidrei for cello and orchestra, op.47. C. Saint-Saëns has dedicated to the cello: a memorable page in his Carnival of the animals, certainly known to many, Il Cigno, whose transcriptions are often performed for cello and piano and for cello and harp; the Allegro Appassionato for cello and piano; the two Concerts for cello and orchestra op. 33 in the min. and op.119 n. 2 in re min., And the sonatas for cello and piano op. 18 n. 1 in d major, op. 32 n. 1, op. 123 n. 2 and the romance for cello and piano op. 67. C. Debussy has written a sonata for cello and piano op. 40. Zoltán Kodály composed the sonatina for cello (1923), a sonata for cello and piano op. 4 and a sonata for cello solo op. 8. B. Britten has composed three Suites for cello solo op. 72, op. 80 and op. 87. P. Il'ič Čajkovskij composed Variations on a Rococo Theme for Cello and Orchestra, op. 33. G. Enescu has composed two sonatas for cello and piano at a distance of thirty-seven years from each other, the first in 1898 op. 26 n. 1 in fa min and the second in 1935 op. 26 n. 2 in do magg. A. Dvořák composed over the extraordinary concert for cello and orchestra op. in si min. and also a sonata for cello and piano in fa magg. of which, however, the last movement remained unfinished.

F. Delius has composed a double concert for violin, cello and orchestra and a sonata for cello and piano in 1916. S. Rachmaninov in 1901 composed a sonata for cello and piano op. 19 in sol min. which is always very appreciated by the public in concerts. S. Prokofiev wrote in 1949 a cello sonata op. 119 in do magg. and piano and the Sinfonia concertante for cello and orchestra op. 125 in mi min. Francis Poulenc wrote in 1948 a sonata for cello and piano op. 143. P. Hindemith has written two sonatas for cello and piano op. 11 n. 3 and one from 1948; also very famous is the cello solo sonata Op. 25 No. 3. In 1882 R. Strauss wrote a sonata for cello and piano op. 6 in fa magg and a Romanza for cello and orchestra. A. Honneger has composed two sonatas for cello and piano H.4 and H.32 in re min. Bertold Hummel has composed two sonatas for cello and piano op. 2 in fa and later in 1955 the Sonata brevis op. 11a. C. Villiers Stanford has composed two sonatas for cello and piano op 9. n. 1 in the major in 1878 and op. 39 n. 2 in re min in 1893. K. Weill composed a sonata for cello and piano in 1920. S. Barber composed a sonata in 1932 for cello and piano op.6 in do min. John Ireland composed a single sonata for cello and piano in 1923. E. Bloch composed: a Symphony for trombone or cello and orchestra, Schelomo Jewish rhapsody for cello and orchestra and the Suite for cello solo. D. Sŏstakovich loved the cello very much and the close friendship that bound him to the great Russian cellist Mstslav Rostropovich certainly contributed to the birth of some of the following masterpieces: the sonata for cello and piano op 119 in do magg. and the two concerts for cello and orchestra op. 107 in mi bem. Maj. of 1959 and op. 126 n. 2 of 1966. Also in 1962 D. Kabalevsky composed a sonata for cello and piano op. 71 in si bem. Maj. The sonata for cello and piano (1978) is known by A. Schnittke; S. Gubaidulina has composed a concerto for cello and orchestra Detto-2 (1972), Dieci preludi for cello solo (1974), In Croce for cello and organ (1979) and for bayan **16.** and cello (1991), Rejoice, violin sonata and violoncello (1981), Sieben Worte for cello, bayan, and strings (1982), The Feast is in Full Procession (И: Празднество в разгаре) for cello and orchestra (1993), The Canticle of the Creatures of St. Francis of Assisi for cello, a cappella choir, and orchestra (1997), Mirage: The Dancing Sun for eight cellos (2002), On the Edge of Abyss for seven cellos and two waterphones **17.** (2002), Verwandlung (Transformation) for trombone, saxophone quartet, cello, double bass, and tam-tam (2004); M. Reger has composed three suites for cello solo op. 131, L. Liebermann has composed four sonatas for cello and piano Op. 3 n.1 (1978), op.61 n. 2 (1998), op. 90 n. 3 (2005), op.108 n. 4 (2008); H. Villa-Lobos has composed two concerts for cello and orchestra; J. Rodrigo has composed a short Sonata for cello and piano in the and two works for cello and orchestra: Concierto en modo galante (1949) Concierto as a fun (1978-1981); I. Xenakis has composed Nomos Alpha for solo cello; A. Piazzolla has composed Le Grand Tango for cello and piano (bandoneon); L. Dallapiccola has composed the Ciaccona for cello, intermezzo and adagio for cello solo. L. Berio wrote in 1977 The return of the Snovidenia for cello and small orchestra and the XIV Sequenza for cello only in 2002.

Cellists of yesterday and today

The possible list of the great virtuosos of this instrument is nourished. Carry forward to follow the names of those who are known to the general public both for their discography, and for their presence in the most prestigious concert halls in the world and who have been honored and awarded in the most illustrious music competitions and who have held and they play the role of cello in the most prestigious orchestras.

Among the greatest virtuosos and masters I want to mention: Pablo Casals, Pierre Fournier, Paul Tortelier, Maurice Gendron, Andres Navarra, Anton Janigro, Danil Shafran, Mstslav Rostropovic, Janos Starker, Jaqueline Du Pré, Zara Nelsova, Siegfried Palm, Natalja Gutman, Myung -Wah Chung, Lynn Harrel, Régis Pasquier, David Geringas, Miša Majskij, Heinrich Schiff, Yo-Yo Ma, Radu Aldulescu, Anton Niculescu, Augustine Lefevbre, Michael Flaksman, Erich Oskar Hutter, Luc Toten, Vadim Pavlov, Alain Meunier, Julian Lloyd Webber, Bailey Zuill, Raphael Wallfisch, Steven Isserliss, Anner Bylsma, Walter Grimer, Giedre Dirvanauskaite, Robert Witt, Daniel Müller-Schott, Jorge Guillermo Schultis, Relja Lukic, Marianne Chen, Kristi Curb; among the Italians, Gilberto Crepax, Benedetto Mazzacurati, Ferdinando Forino, Aldo Pais, Luigi Chiarappa, Enrico Mainardi, Giuseppe Selmi, Franco Rossi, Rocco Filippini, Arturo Bonucci, Mario Brunello, Enrico Dindo, Amedeo Baldovino, Franco

Maggio Ormezosky, Francesco Strano, Giovanni Sollima, Sandro Laffranchini, Massimo Polidori, Marco Scano, Enrico Bronzi, Antonio Mosca, Matteo Tabbia, Luigi Piovano, Gabriele Geminiani, Emanuele Galanti, Emanuele Silvestri, Alessandro Zanardi, Claudio Marini, Luca Signorini, Marco Severi, Andrea Noferini, Giorgio Gasbarro .

ADDITIONAL NOTES

1. François Adrien Servais (Hal, Bruxelles, 1807-66) Belgian cellist and composer. A pupil of J. N. Plantel, he began a brilliant concert career in 1834 which made him famous throughout Europe. He composed fantasies, concerts and duets for his instrument, but he is remembered above all for his contributions to the cellist technique. The "Paganini of the cello" was defined by Berlioz. Musicians were the sons Joseph (1850-85), cellist, and François-Mathieu (1846-1901), conductor.

2. Violone is an ancient and obsolete musical instrument of the group of chordophones, it belongs to the family of the bowed instruments and to the subfamily of the "violas" which includes ancient instruments with "C" cuts, tuned for intervals of fourth and third, with strings in number varying from three to six or seven or more. In the subfamily of the violets, the violone is the one that has the largest dimensions and has the most severe texture. It is a six-stringed instrument (although there are some models that have 5 or more rarely 4 strings) with keys, usually tuned a fifth or an octave below the bass of viola. The violone can be defined as a double bass instrument because its texture includes sounds that are more serious than those of the bass weaving of a family of instruments

3. Violoncino, is an instrument very similar to a small cello used between 1580 and 1750 that fulfilled the role of tenor that could have 4 or 5 strings:

from the acute mi-la-re-sol-do, mi- la-re-sol or more rarely the same tuning as the cello. It sounds similar to the cello. This instrument was confused with the small cello. For this latter type of instrument they composed G. B. Sammartini a C major concerto for small cello and string orchestra and J. S. Bach used it in numerous cantatas such as: Bleib bei uns, denn es will Abend werden (BWV 6); Jesu, nun sei gepreiset (BWV 41); Ich geh und suche mit Verlangen (BWV 49) Also hat Gott die Welt geliebt (BWV 68) Gott ist mein König (BWV 71) Ich bin e guter Hirt (BWV 85) Mache dich, mein Geist, bereit (BWV 115) Er rufet seinen Schafen mit Namen (BWV 175) Schmücke dich, o liebe Seele (BWV 180) Sie werden euch in den Bann tun (BWV 183) Mein Herze schwimmt im Blut (BWV 199)

4. **Fontana Giovanni Battista,** known as "dal Violino" (Brescia, second half of the 16th century - Padua 1630) violinist and composer. He served in S. Maria delle Grazie in Brescia and later in Venice, Rome and Padua, much appreciated as a violinist. He published a collection of six sonatas in one, two, three, stylistically close to those of B. Marini, of which he was probably a teacher.

5. **Lauro Malusi**, Il Violoncello, Zanibon (1973).

6. **Marin Mersenne**, Harmonie Universelle , Paris, 1636-37; Partial English traslatino of Roger E. Chapman in Harmonie Universelle, the Books of Instruments, L'Aia, 1957. [N. d.] Facsimile Ed. by Francois Lesure, Paris, 1963. [N. D.]

7. William Pleeth: a great performer, in a group and as a soloist, techer for thirty years, from 1948 to 1978, he gave the cello course at the Guildhall School of Music and Drama in London; he became famous for his extraordinary interpretative wisdom.

8. Nona Pyron: British cellist of International renown: in particolar he explored the oldest reperto ire, which he performer on ancient original instruments.

9. Marin Mersenne, op. cit.Proposition I.

10. Marin Mersenne, op. cit.

11. Consort is a term that indicates a group of instruments; whole consort is made up of instruments of the same family, broken consort by tools of different genres. [N.d.T.]

12. Giovanni Maria Bononcini (Buononcini) (1642-1678) born of a violinist and composer father: active at the Modena court, he had written a treatise, Musico prattico, published in 1673. Giovanni's younger brother, Antonio Maria, was also a musician .It was from his father that he received his first musical education; when he died, in 1678, he became a student of Giovanni Paolo Colonna in Bologna, where his first works were performed. Thanks to Colonna he became part of the Accademia dei Filarmonici as a composer. In 1685 he had already prepared and published his first works. In 1688 he obtained the post of musician at the basilica of San Petronio, and later became maestro di cappella in the church of San Giovanni in Monte. From 1692 he went to Milan, Rome (where he was appreciated and supported by Filippo II Colonna and his consort Olimpia Pamphilj) and Venice; finally, from 1698 to 1711 he settled in Vienna, where he enjoyed the favors of the emperors Leopold I and Joseph I. Passing through Berlin in 1702, he met Georg Friedrich Händel, five years younger than him, whose early talent he recognized: he would meet again some years later.From 1714 to 1719 he was again in Rome, in the service of Johann Wenzel, Count of Gallas. Then, from 1720 he settled in London, under the protection of John Churchill, 1st Duke of Marlborough. Here he also performed on the cello in numerous concerts, much appreciated by the English aristocracy. The most successful works of Bononcini in those years were Astarto (1720), Crispo (1722), Griselda (1722), which turned out to be a real triumph, Erminia (1723), Calfurnia (1724). In favor of the Italian there was also a certain hostility towards Händel due to his German origins and to the contemporary presence on the English throne of the little-loved Hanoverian dynasty. But in 1727-1728 a scandal broke out which compromised the success of Bononcini and forced him to leave London: the composer Antonio Lotti accused the Bononcini madrigal In a shady hedge of being a plagiarism of an excerpt of his Duetti, trio and madrigals.Having fled to Paris in 1733, due to unfortunate speculation, Bononcini was almost ruined, and he had to make a living by being a copyist. In 1741 he decided to return to Vienna, where he managed to obtain a pension from the empress Maria Theresa of Habsburg. There he died in poverty a few years later.

13. Domenico Gabrielli (Bologna, 19 October 1659 - Bologna, 10 July 1690) was an Italian composer and cellist. In life he was nicknamed Minghino del cello, as in the Bolognese dialect (Mingéin dal viulunzèl) Mingéin is a diminutive of Domenico. He studied composition in Venice with Giovanni Legrenzi and Petronio Franceschini cello. When the latter died, on 20 December 1680 Gabrielli succeeded him as cellist of the chapel of the Basilica of San Petronio in Bologna. On 23 April 1676 he was admitted to the Bologna Philharmonic Academy and in 1683 he became its president. During the 1980s he became famous both as a cello virtuoso and as a vocal music composer. he was forced to renounce the duties that saw him engaged even in San Petronio. These continuous absences were perpetuated until October 14, 1687 when he decided to resign for a few months. After staying for some time in Modena he was reinstated in the staff of the Bolognese cathedral, but contracted a disease which, two years later, led him to morte.Nell 1682 he made his debut as an opera, an activity that will see him engaged for at least seven years and that will produce 12 works, mostly written originally for the theaters of Venice, Turin and Modena. In the latter city he was also often employed in his cello performances at the Este court, so much so that he was often forced to renounce the duties that saw him engaged in San Petronio as well. These continuous absences were perpetuated until October 14, 1687 when he decided to resign for a few months. After staying for some time in Modena, he was reinstated in the staff of the Bolognese cathedral, but contracted a disease which, two years later, led to his death.

14.Giuseppe Maria Jacchini (Bologna 1667-1727) composer and cellist. Member of the Bologna Philharmonic Academy, renowned cellist of the chapel of San Petronio, he was among the first to use the cello as a solo instrument in the form of the concert. In his production the Concerti for chamber with three and four instruments stand out with obligatory cello op. 4 (1701) and the Sonatas for cello solo, for violin and cello, for cello and bass.

15. Attilio Ariosti (Bologna, November 5, 1666 - London, 1729) was an Italian composer. Attilio Ariosti, born in 1666, became a monk at the age of 22, undertook the study of the cello and later became an organist in the church of S. Maria dei Servi in Bologna. In 1694 he composed "Divertimento da chamber a violino e cello" and two years later he collaborated on the pastoral drama "Il Tirsi" and composed the "Daphne", then he asked and obtained permission to leave the order to work as a Duke's court composer of Mantua. In 1697 he moved to Berlin at the request of the Princess of Prussia where he became music teacher of the Electrix of Brandenburg; his last Berlin work was "Mars and Irene" from 1703. Having been recalled to Italy, he left Berlin and stopped in Vienna until 1711 where he composed many works, from the musical entertainment "The glorious omens of the African Scipio" of 1704 until the dramatic poem "La Placidia" and the "Passion of Christ" and was General Agent of Austria for Italy. Back in Italy, he was expelled and expatriated, in 1716, to England, where he obtained great success and where he published the "Collection of Cantatas, and Lessons for the Viola d'Amour". [1] Writer mainly of works, Attilio Ariosti is currently remembered as one of the most important composers for the Viola d'Amore for whom he left in addition to the aforementioned "Collection" also a series of scattered movements, gathered under the name "Sonatas of Stockholm", seen that the manuscript is found in the Statens Musikbibliotek in Stockholm

16. Bayan: chromatic button accordion, developed in Russia at the beginning of the 20th century

17. Waterphones: a unique type of atonal acoustic musical instrument built largely with stainless steel resonator "bowl" with a cylindrical "neck", containing a small amount of water and with brass rods around the rim of the bowl. Several sizes and design variants of the tool are available. It is generally played in a position set by a soloist and is played by bending or drumming and movement so as to affect the water inside and thus in the sound characteristics of the bowl and the rods. The waterphone is recognized as a true musical instrument and appears in film recordings, record albums and is used in live performances. As in the "ambient music genre", there is no established notation established for mapping compositions. The waterphone is a modern invention inspired by "the Tibetan water drum, a round, slightly flattened, bronze, drum with an opening in the center top," according to the inventor of the waterphone, Richard A. Waters . The waterphone partly revives the sound-producing principle of an earlier instrument called a nail violin, which also used a resonator and rods (nails) and was hit or bent. Contemporary classical composers who have written parts for the waterphone in compositions include Sofia Gubaidulina, Tan by Tan, Christopher Rouse, Carson Cooman, Andi Spicer, Andrew Carter and Todd Barton. It has also been used prominently by rock musicians Richard Barone and Alex Wong (when playing with Vienna Teng) and can be heard in music from the pocket of the harmonica.

BIBLIOGRAPHY

- AMADEUS SPECIAL of February 1995, JOHANN SEBASTIAN BACH
- Italian origins of Adriano Cavicchi

- GHIGI MARCELLA, The violoncello. Know the technique to express music, Milan, Casa Musicale Sonzogno, 1999

- DICTIONARY OF MUSIC AND MUSICIANS, Grove George 1984

- DINDO GIANFRANCO, Guide to Violin Making, Franco Muzio Editore, Padua 1991

- DIOLI ARRIGO, Cello Art in Italy, Music Editions A L G A, Ferrara 1969

- UNIVERSAL ENCYCLOPEDIC DICTIONARY OF MUSIC AND MUSICIANS, U.T.E.T. 1982

- ENCICLOPEDIA DELLA MUSICA, Garzanti 1998

- INTERNATIONAL THREE-YEAR BODY OF THE INSTRUMENTS OF THE ARCH AND THE LIUTA CONSORTIUM ANTONIO STRADIVARI DI CREMONA, The cellos by Antonio Stradivari, Silvana Editoriale 2003

- FARGA FRANZ, History of the violin, Corbaccio from Oglio Editore

- FORINO LUIGI, Il violoncello, Ulrico Hoepli Publisher bookseller of Real Casa, Milan 1930

- MALUSI LAURA, The bow of musical instruments, Zanibon Editions, Milan 1981

- PASQUALI GIULIO - PRINCE REMY, Il violino, Edizioni Curci, Milan 1951

- PLEETH WILLIAM, Il violoncello, Franco Muzio Editore, Padua 1989

- REGAZZI ROBERTO, The Complete Luthier's Library. A Useful International Critical Bibliography for the Maker and the Connoisseur of Stringed and Plucked Instruments by Bologna: Florenus, 1990

- SACHS CURT, History of musical instruments, Einaudi EditionsTurin 1996

- WILLIAM SANDYS History of the Violin, by and Simon Andrew, Dover Publications, 2006.

INDEX

Made in United States
Troutdale, OR
09/13/2024

22776923R00033